THE POEMS OF DOCTOR ZHIVAGO

THE POEMS OF DOCTOR ZHIVAGO

Translated from the Russian

by Eugene M. Kayden

With an Introduction by James Morgan

Illustrated by Bill Greer

♛ HALLMARK CROWN EDITIONS

THE LIFE OF DOCTOR ZHIVAGO

Wind whistles across the Russian plain, whipping snow into
tiny whirlwinds. Trees bend like switches in the stinging air.
Night settles upon the countryside, and for miles all is icy
and dark except for one small patch of yellow light in a window.
Inside the house sits Yuri Zhivago, poet and former doctor.
A pad of blank paper rests on the table before him.
And as the dim light from the single candle dances upon his face,
Zhivago gazes at the empty bed where last night his lover slept.
Lara is gone now, and life is no longer for living—
only for re-living in the lines of poems
written in a small room in a house on the Russian plain.

In his youth, Zhivago is an orphan raised by a cultured Moscow family in an upper-class Moscow home, his mind on music and medicine, fine art and literature. Some of his countrymen find life hard, but for Zhivago the storm of upheaval is drowned out by the strains of a symphony orchestra.

Then comes World War I, and later the Revolution. By this time Zhivago has married his childhood sweetheart and become a father. He leaves wife and child for the front to serve as medical officer in the Russian army. His nurse is a woman he has seen twice before and never forgotten. ...*Your image...*/*Is now in silver lines*/*Cut deep within my heart...* Once Zhivago accompanied another doctor to her house. Later she interrupted a Christmas party by shooting her lover. Her name is Lara, and for almost two years they work together, side by side, amid the sickness and the death. It is a time of revelation for Zhivago. War is a new experience, and so is Lara. Zhivago remembers his wife Tonia—cultured, refined, fragile. Lara is of the earth—fresh, warm, strong. Outside, the Revolution rages. Inside Zhivago, a more personal kind of revolution begins to burn.

Going home after the war, Zhivago reflects on all he has seen. It will be good to return to *life,* he thinks, to pick it up where he left it, to get settled once again in the warmth and peacefulness that he had known before the war. And as the train rumbles onward across the wide, dark land toward home, Zhivago's thoughts drift also to Lara. She is stranded God knows where by the devastating war. She may have no future, and yet she is strong, silent, reserved. ...A *shining wisp of hair / Lights suddenly your face...* His desire not to love her is as strong as his desire to love his family and his friends.

But life in Moscow disappoints Zhivago. At first he had welcomed the Revolution. Now, when his life becomes restricted by the Communists, Zhivago rebels. He has seen enough of war and suffering to make him know the value of life for life's sake, of freedom and the right to go about one's business. After a hard winter in Moscow, then, he packs up his family and moves away from the city to Varykino, Tonia's family estate near the Ural Mountains, not far from a town called Yuriatin.

The move to Varykino marks the beginning of Zhivago's rebirth. It is a time of awakening, of new life, free, clean, pure, and happy. "Back to the land," says Tonia, and indeed they *are* back, back to an honest life of working with their hands, of planting a garden and living off the soil. ...*The tines of pitchforks glow with health / Freed from their winter rust and stains...* Zhivago gives up medicine and gives himself over to poetry. And he spends much time reading, pouring over Pushkin, Stendhal, Dickens, while Tonia knits in front of the stove and their son Sasha plays before them on the floor.

When chores permit, Zhivago travels to the nearby

town of Yuriatin to visit the public library there. One day about a year after his arrival at Varykino, as he sits thumbing through a book of Russian history, he notices a reader on the other side of the room. Her back is to him, but he recognizes her immediately. It is Lara.

All that time with her in the war, nearly two years, and he had tried to deny it, to put it out of his mind and pretend that it had not happened. Yet here again they are thrown together. Like Romeo and Juliet, they are star-crossed—destined, it seems, to become lovers.

Zhivago finds with Lara a happiness he has never known before. She is a kindred spirit, and their moments together blossom with discovery. He loves Tonia still, but Lara becomes the great love of Zhivago's life. Zhivago's story recounts man's struggle against the forces of history, against a universe which dooms man to run and hide from life like a rat in the street. Zhivago personifies man's hope that there is something better, and it is Lara who inspires him.

When Red partisans capture Zhivago as he heads home from Yuriatin, it is to Lara that he later returns, hungry, tired, battered, sick. ...*You are my gift of life when days grow baneful...* He has been held for three years, made to serve as physician to the partisan troops, made to ride with them through three dark, bitter Russian winters. When he finally escapes to Yuriatin, he finds that the civil war has taken its toll there. Its sickness has infected the air of his once idyllic retreat. Lara is waiting for him, but Tonia is gone, forced by war and grief to return to Moscow. The pain he has tried all his life to escape is catching up with him.

By the end of the summer, Zhivago has regained his health. Winter approaches, and with it comes news that changes are taking place in the partisan hierarchy, changes that put Zhivago and Lara in great danger. Zhivago has flaunted the system long enough, and he is marked for extinction. Komarovsky, the man Lara wounded at that Christmas party so many years before, offers them escape. But Zhivago refuses, and Lara will not go without him. "Let's be mad," she says, "if there is nothing except madness left to us." And so it must be. ...*We made / No vows to cross all obstacles, / And so we'll simply face our end...* Tired, desperate, frightened—beaten but refusing to admit defeat—they steal away through the night to the only place left—Varykino.

There they spend the last days of their brief time together, making a home in two rooms of the old house, living happily in the last hours before the final darkness. It is an icy Eden from which they know they must go, and they live all the more intensely because of it. In the daytime they are together. At night when Lara sleeps, Zhivago sits at a little table by the window, a single candle flickering, and he writes as he had always wished to write. His poems are about life and death, about God

and fate and man and the hopes of one now about to be destroyed. And they are about Lara. ...*The universal sphere was like a soundless waste / And only the garden spot was warm with life...* His imagination soars! The life he has known and the life he has wanted to know flood freely upon the page with visions of rich earth and fertility, of "the smell of life-begetting dung," of a world "hard as stone." Through all his poems runs the assertion of the value of life, of beauty, of nature. Zhivago is a man caught between two realities — the reality of history, of the every-day world and the reality of his own poetic vision. Even

9

at the end, with the realities of history crashing down around him, Zhivago clings to his view of life and claims the ultimate victory:

> "I will suffer death and on the third day rise,
> And, as rafts come floating down a river,
> Like a caravan of sails, the centuries
> Will come to me for judgment from the dark."

Soon Komarovsky comes to tell them that time is short. Lara still refuses to leave alone, and so Zhivago tells her to go ahead, that he will follow soon. It is decided. They kiss good-bye and Lara gets into the sleigh beside Komarovsky. It is late afternoon when she leaves, and the shadows shift blue-gray on the snow as Zhivago watches the sleigh become a speck in the distance. They are never to be together again.

The wind rustles lightly in black branches, and a chill hangs in the air. Time is suspended for a moment in his gaze. When he can no longer see her, Zhivago turns and walks back inside the empty house to write his poems about Lara and a life of shattered dreams.

THE POEMS OF DOCTOR ZHIVAGO

HAMLET

The plaudits slowly fade away.
Again I come upon the stage.
I strain to hear in dying echoes
The fate that waits our present age.

Through thousands of binoculars
The night of darkness stares at me.
If possible, O Abba, Father,
Then take away this cup from me.

I love Thy stern design, and I am
Content to act this role of woe.
But there's another play on stage;
Then spare me now, and let me go.

The acts are plotted, planned with care;
The end, foredoomed. I stand alone.
The Pharisees exult in pride.
O hard the way--our ways of stone.

13

MARCH

The earth is steaming, drenched in sweat;
Ravines run dazed and turbulent.
Like a bustling milkmaid hard at work,
Spring labors long, is well content.

The scanty snows now sick and helpless
Lie prone, with branching bluish veins.
The tines of pitchforks glow with health,
Freed from their winter rust and stains.

O nights, O passing days and nights!
The drip from eaves and window sills,
The thinning icicles on gables,
The chatter of unsleeping rills!

The pigeons peck at oats in snow
About the sheds and stables flung
Wide open, and vaster than spring air
The smell of life-begetting dung.

HOLY WEEK

The dark of night lies everywhere.
So young the night around,
We see how vast with stars the sky,
Each star as radiant as day.
And if the earth could have its way,
It would sleep on—through Easter Day—
Lulled by the reading of the psalms.

The dark of night lies everywhere.
So young the night, the square seems like
Eternity from end to end
Where still a thousand years must wait
The dawn of day and light.

The earth is naked to the bone:
It hasn't got a thread to wear
For swinging chapel bells
Or singing with the choir.

From Maundy Thursday
Unto the eve of Easter Day,
The waters gnaw at riverbanks
And swirl in pools and breakers.

The woods are also naked
And hushed through Passiontide;
The pines stand crowded in a throng
Like worshippers at prayer.

And in the city, rallied about
The square, the thronging trees
Stand in their nakedness, and peer
Through gratings at the church.

They gaze with awe. Their alarm
And fears are justified;
The gardens leave their fences,
Degrees and laws of life are rent—
For God is given to the grave.

They see the light at the royal gate,
The tapers glowing, the black pall,
The faces stained with tears.
They see the long procession starting
With Cross and Shroud
And that two birches at the gate
Have bowed aside to let them pass.

They move around the cloister walls
In crowds from curb to curb,
And bring the spring into the church—
The voice of spring,
The heady fumes of spring,
The springtime of the air,
Pungent as a holy wafer.

March scatters handfuls of the snow
Like alms among the lame,
As though a man had carried out
The holy Ark outside the church,
And gave its all unto the poor.

They sing until the sunrise hour.
Then, having wept their fill,
Their chants of the Psalms and Acts
Flow with an air serene
Into an empty lamplit street.

All creatures hear the voice of spring
In the still of night, believing
That when good weather comes
Death itself shall be destroyed
By the travail of the Resurrection.

WHITE NIGHT

I dream of a night long ago
And a house on the Petersburg Quai.
A poor landowner's daughter, you came
As a student alone to the city.

You are comely, admired by many,
So many. You and I, that evening,
Sit snug at your window, watching
The street from your attic room.

There, lamps like butterflies flicker
In the chill of morning rays.
I speak to you softly—of matters
Still at rest in far-away time.

We dream we are bound together
By a feeling of timid devotion
To a mystery that holds our city
On the shores of the boundless Neva.

We hear, far among dark copses,
In the silvery evening of spring,
The nightingales trill and whistle
Triumphant in revels of song.

The song of each singer, the frenzy
Of tremulous chirping and trilling,
Awakens unrest and delight
In the depths of spell-bound groves.

And Night, like a barefoot pilgrim,
Secretly creeps by the fences,
Trailing behind her the wraith
Of our words from the window-sill.

In the cadence of echoing words
Overheard, in the gardens about,
The apple and cherry tree branches
In shining white blossoms appear.

Like luminous phantoms the trees
Come thronging out on the highway —
To wave their farewell to Night
That knows what is fated to be.

SPRING FLOODS

The sunset flames were dying down.
Along spring-flooded forest trails
A weary horseman slowly rode
Toward a lonely Ural mountain farm.

The horse came, panting, all in sweat.
The churning streams along the road
Pursued the horseman, echoing
The swish and splash of hoofs in slush.

But when the rider loosed his reins
And slowed his horse down to a walk,
The spring floods thundered by his side
In all their gathered clash and roar.

There someone mocked, and someone wept,
And stone was ground to dust on stone.
The loosened and uprooted stumps
Tumbled into the swirling tides.

Against the sunset conflagration,
Among the charcoal branches flung
In space, the frenzied nightingale
Raged like a booming tocsin bell.

And where the weeping willow plunged
Her widow's veil above a hollow,
It whistled in the seven oak trees
Like the Robber-Nightingale of old.

What hopeless passion or misfortune
Foretold this frenzied, glowing song?
At whom the whistling singer aimed
This flying grapeshot in the woods?

It seemed that from a convicts' hide-out
A demon of the woods might rise
To meet the horse or foot patrols
Of partisans from local posts.

The earth and sky, the field and forest
Gave heed to each unique, fine tone,
Each measured note of sheerest madness,
Deep anguish, happiness, or pain.

EXPLANATION

Life has returned no matter how,
As once—no matter why—it snapped.
I live in the same old-fashioned street
As in that summer, on that day.

The folks, the same; their cares, the same.
The sunset flames still faintly glow
Where the night of death had nailed them
In haste on the walls of Manége Square.

The women in shabby cotton dresses
Still saunter down the square at night,
And are, as then, still crucified
In attic rooms beneath tin roofs.

There one of them appears inside
Her doorway, dragging slow her feet,
Climbs slowly from her basement cave
And cuts obliquely through the yard.

Again I'm ready with excuses
As one unmindful of the world.
I'm glad that next-door woman skirts
The alley, leaving us alone.

Oh, do not weep! Do not pucker
Your swollen lips again,
For that would only crack the scab
Made by the fevered spring.

Hands off my breast, I say! We're like
Live wires; the current's on.
We shall again be thrown together,
Unawares, against our will.

Yes, you'll marry, then forget
The hardships of the past.
A woman's life is a noble quest
And trust—that drives men mad.

As for me, I have stood lifelong
In devotion, in reverence
Before the miracle of woman—
Her throat, shoulders, hands.

No matter how the night may weld
Its chain of grief with longing new,
No power is stronger than the passion
That also pulls our lives apart.

SUMMER IN THE CITY

They whisper in silence.
With an impetuous air
She sweeps up from her neck
Her tumbling hair.

Like a helmeted woman,
She peers out from behind
The encircling strands
That fall from her comb.

But the night is seared
With its heat and grime.
The loiterers scamper
To get home on time.

From afar the thunder
Comes suddenly near,

And the window curtains
Flap trembling with fear.

Deep silence. The air is
Still muggy with heat;
Then flashes of lightning,
And scurrying feet.

When morning flames out
In a blaze again,
And the sun dries clean
The puddles of rain,

Old lime trees awaken
To a freshness deep,
Unfaded, sweet-scented,
All heavy with sleep.

WINDS

I have died. You live alone with woe.
Now stormwinds, keening and repining,
Rock house and pine trees to and fro—
Not tree by tree, but at one blow
All groves together intertwining
With the illimitable space.
Thus sailboats sheltered at their base
Are rocked by winds along a bay.
But not in senseless agitation
The stormwind rages day by day:
Alone of grief its lamentation
And for you its lullaby of desolation.

INTOXICATION

Neath a willow with ivy entangled
We take cover in blustery weather.
My arms are wreathed about you;
In my raincape we huddle together.

I was wrong: Not ivy, my dearest,
But hops encircle this willow.
Well, then, let's spread in its shelter
My cape for a rug and a pillow!

INDIAN SUMMER

The leaves of the currants are coarse.
Amid laughter and clatter of jars,
The women are shredding, preserving,
And pickling with pepper and cloves.

Like a jester, the copse hurls headlong
Their hubbub far down a cliff
Where the hazels lie scorched in the sun
As if seared by old campfire flames.

A path leads down to the gully
Where, among dry stumps and snags,
You feel sorry for Autumn, who sweeps
To the gully old rubbish and scrap;

Sorry, too, that creation is simpler
Than some clever chatterers think;
That the copses are sunk in morasses,
And that everything's fated to die;

That there is no sense in your staring
Because nature is shriveled by heat,
That the cobweb threads of Autumn
Drift in through the windows as ash.

There's a path through the garden fence
And a trail to a copse of birches.
There's laughter and noise in the house,
Like the hubbub far down the cliff.

THE WEDDING PARTY

All the guests at evening came
To the wedding feast
For the marriage songs and dancing
Nightlong in the yard.

After midnight until seven
From the wedded couple
Not a whisper reached the crowd
Through their bedroom door.

But at early dawn when sleep is
Sweet with dreaming, dreaming,
The accordion sang out again
At the parting hour.

The harmonicas played loudly
One more merry tune
To the clapping and the stamping
Of the dancing guests.

Then again, again the ringing
Snatches of gay song
Burst upon the sleepers' bed
From the merry crowd.

There a wench, as white as snow,
Like a peahen glided,
Swaying softly, while the dancers
Whistled, whooped, and yelled.

Tossing jauntily her head,
Her right hand awaving,
Like a peahen, like a peahen,
Trippingly she danced.

Suddenly all noise and shouting
And the swing of song
Faded into silence—faded
With the dying night.

Soon the yard awakened
With the rush of chores,
With busy morning chatter
And with peals of laughter.

In a whirlwind of gray patches
Flocks of pigeons rose,
Soaring high above the dovecotes
In the boundless blue.

Surely someone, on awaking,
Came to set them free
With a greeting cry for happy,
Happy wedded years.

Life is thus a moment only,
Only a dissolving
Of ourselves in other selves
As a hearty gift.

Life is but a wedding gift
Bursting from the light, —
Like a song, a dream, a pigeon
Winging in the blue.

AUTUMN

I've given leave to all who're dear
And near to me to go their way.
The world is empty; in my heart
I feel my lifelong loneliness.

We're now together in this lodge,
Alone. The forest is deserted.
As in our ancient songs, the trails
Run wild in brambles and in weeds.

The timbered walls in quiet sadness
Regard both you and me. We made
No vows to cross all obstacles,
And so we'll simply face our end.

We'll meet at one — I with a book,
And you with your embroidery;
We shall forget at break of day
How long our kissing in the night.

Let leaves spin headlong down, ablaze
In glory, splendid in their death,
And swell our cup of bitter grief
And anguish deeper day by day.

Let stormwinds strew as leaves afar
Our life, devotion, beauty, joy!
Like a leaf in autumn, drift away,
Go half insane, out, out of sight!

Yet as the coppice flings its leaves
Upon the air, you loose your dress,
And, in your silken dressing-gown,
You fall into my waiting arms.

You are my gift of life when days
Grow baneful, worse than the disease;
Heroic life is the root of beauty,
And it draws together you and me.

A FAIRY TALE

Once upon a time
In a wonderland
A knight made his way
Through a barren steppe.

As he sped to battle,
He beheld a forest
Loom afar in space
In the heaving dust.

A foreboding clutched
His troubled heart:
Make tight the saddle!
Shun the water hole!

But the fearless knight
Spurned the warning voice
As he rode full speed
Up the wooded hill;

Then across a meadow
To a dried-up stream,
Then around a hill
To a narrow valley;

Through a murky hollow,
By a forest trail
He came at noontide
To the water hole.

Deaf to every fear
And the warning voice,
Down a steep he led
His thirsting horse.

By the winding stream
Across the shallow
Eerie flames sprang high
Above a yawning cave.

Through blinding smoke
And brimstone flames
A shrill cry rang out
Within towering pines.

The rider, startled,
Pressed bravely on
Through a long ravine—
Toward the call for help.

He beheld the dragon
And he gripped his lance;
He beheld its head,
Its tail, and scales.

The dragon darted
Red shafts of flame.
In three coils it circled
A maiden form.

The serpent's neck
Swung like a whip
Across the victim's
Head and shoulders.

Every year by custom
To that forest monster
Was sacrificed
A maiden's life.

This was the tribute
The people had to pay
To save their homes
From the serpent's wrath.

The dragon encircled
Her arms and throat—
She, men's tribute
And their sacrifice.

The knight lifted up
A prayer to heaven,
And he couched his lance
For the bitter fight.

Eyes shut in darkness.
High mountains. Clouds.
Fords. Waters. Rivers.
Centuries and years.

The knight fell wounded
On the bloody ground.
His charger trampled
The serpent in the dust.

There horse and dragon
Side by side lay dead;
The knight—unconscious,
The maid—in a trance.

The noontide skies
Shone soft and blue.
Who was she? A princess,
Or a peasant maid?

Her tears ran streaming
From excess of joy,
But she sank again
In a trance of sleep.

Then the knight awakened,
Too weak to move,
From his waste of strength,
From the loss of blood.

Their hearts were beating
As by swelling waves;
They sank, or wakened—
Only to sleep again.

Eyes shut in darkness.
High mountains. Clouds.
Fords. Waters. Rivers.
Centuries and years.

AUGUST

As promised, faithfully and free
The sun spread wide its morning rays
As a slant-wise beam of saffron light
From window curtains to my couch.

It spattered with its sultry ochre
The village houses and the grove,
My dampened pillow and my bed,
The bookshelf, and a bit of wall.

I then remembered why my pillow
Felt dampened somewhat from my tears.
I dreamed you came for a last farewell,
That you trailed behind me in the woods.

You trailed in groups, or came in pairs;
That someone in the crowd recalled
It was the holy sixth of August,
The transfiguration of our Lord.

That on this day Mount Tabor shines
In clear pure light without a flame;
That, like an oriflamme in brightness,
Autumn draws closer every heart.

You too came through the beggared scrub,
Through sparse and stunted alder trees,
To reach the coppice and the church
Bright-flaring as a ginger bunny.

The sky was like a next-door neighbor
Sedate above unruffled treetops.
And far away the air sang long
With roosters interchanging calls.

Death hovered like a state surveyor
Inside the cloistered graveyard, scanning
Reflectively my dull dead face—
How best to dig my grave to size.

Each one, in every sense and feeling,
Heard inwardly a quiet voice,
My prophetic voice of days ago
That rang unsullied by corruption:

"Farewell, O day of azure and of gold
Upon the Lord's Transfiguration!
O comfort with a woman's last caress
The grief of my predestined hour!

"Farewell, O days of dull despair!
O woman, challenging all wrongs
And degradation, now we part! —
I am the stage of all your struggles.

"Farewell, O winged imagination
And daring flights in life made free,
And worlds made manifest in words,
In thought, in miracles of art."

WINTER NIGHT

The snow was falling, falling slow
From land to land.
A candle flamed upon a table;
A candle flamed.

As midges of the summer swarm
Against a flame,
Outside the snowflakes swarmed against
The windowpane.

The blizzard modelled on the glass
White spheres and arrows.
A candle flamed upon a table;
A candle flamed.

And soft along the lighted ceiling
Shadows lingered:
Shadows of crossed arms, crossed legs,
Crossed destinies.

Two little shoes fell to the floor,
Fell with a thud.
The candle shed its waxen tears
Upon a dress.

The world in snowy darkness lay,
In grey-white mist.
A candle flamed upon a table;
A candle flamed.

A draft then shuddered in the flame.
The fever of temptation
Raised up the cross of angel wings
Upon a wall.

Day after day through February
The snow came down.
A candle flamed upon a table;
A candle flamed.

PARTING

He stands and stares across the hall
And does not know his home.
Her sudden leaving was a flight,
With chaos left behind.

He does not try to comprehend
The chaos in the room,
Because his headache makes him faint,
And tears make dim his eyes.

A throbbing pain rings in his ears.
Is he awake or dreaming?
And why so constant in his mind
The vision of the sea?

When you no longer see the world
Behind hoar-frosted panes,
The hopelessness of sorrow seems
Greater than the lonely sea.

And yet he drew her close to him,
One dear in every feature,
As the shores are closer to the sea
With each inflowing tide.

As reeds sink downward in a storm
With seas in agitation,
Her traits and graceful air sank deep
Within his secret soul.

Through all the hardest years of trial,
And utter wretchedness,
Borne up by tides of destiny,
She reached to him for help.

Amid the endless obstacles
And perils of the sea,
The waves had borne her on, but near,
And nearer to him still.

And now her sudden flight—perhaps
Not by her choice at all.
This parting may bring on new grief
And suffering unto death.

He looks around the room again.
In the hurry of her leaving,
She left her dresser disarranged,
Each drawer turned inside out.

He paces up and down in darkness,
He stoops, keeps putting back
The scattered scraps of careful sewing
And patterns in their places.

And bending o'er a strip of her
Unfinished needlework,
He sees the whole of her in life
And weeps in silence, softly.

MEETING

The snow will bury roads
And houses to the roofs.
If I go to stretch my legs,
I see you at my door.

In a light fall coat, alone,
Without overshoes or hat,
You try to keep your calm,
Sucking your snow-wet lips.

The trees and fences draw
Far back into the gloom.
You watch the street, alone
Within the falling snow.

Your scarf hangs wet with snow,
Your collar and your sleeves,
And stars of melted flakes
Gleam dewy in your hair.

A shining wisp of hair
Lights suddenly your face,
Your figure in the cold,
In that thin overcoat.

Flakes gleam beneath your lashes.
And anguish in your eyes.
You were created whole,
A seamless shape of love.

It seems as if your image
Drawn fine with pointed steel
Is now in silver lines
Cut deep within my heart.

Forever there you live
In your true humility.
It does not really matter
If the world is hard as stone.

I feel I am your double,
Like you outside, in dark.
I cannot draw the line
Dividing you from me.

For who are we, and whence,
If their idle talk alone
Lives long in aftertime
When we no longer live?

STAR OF THE NATIVITY

It was wintertime.
The wind was blowing from the plains.
And the infant was cold in the cave
On the slope of a hill.

He was warmed by the breath of an ox.
Every farmyard beast
Huddled safe in the cave;
A warm mist drifted over the manger.

On a rock afar some drowsy shepherds
Shook off the wisps of straw
And hayseed of their beds,
And sleepily gazed into the vast of night.

They saw gravestones, fences, fields,
The shafts of a cart
Deep in drifted snows,
And a sky of stars above the graveyard.

And, shyer than a watchman's light,
One star alone
Unseen until then
Shone bright on the way to Bethlehem.

At times it rose, a haystack aflame,
Apart from God and the sky,
Like a barn set on fire,
Like a farmstead ablaze in the night.

It reared in the sky like a flaming stack
Of thatch and hay,
In the midst of Creation
Surprised by this new star in the world.

The flame grew steadily deeper, wider,
Large as a portent.
Three stargazers then
Hastened to follow this marvelous light.

Behind them, their camels with gifts;
Their caparisoned asses, each one smaller
In size, came daintily down the hillside.

And all new matters of ages to come
Arose as a vision of wonder in space.
All thoughts of ages, all dreams, new worlds,
All the future of galleries and of museums,
All the games of fairies, the work of inventors,
The yule trees, and the dreams all children dream,
The tremulous glow of candles in rows,

The gold and silver of angels and globes
(A *wind blew, raging, long from the plain*)
And the splendor of tinsel and toys under trees.

A part of the pond lay hidden by alders;
A part could be seen afar from the cliff
Where rooks were nesting among the treetops.
The shepherds could see each ass and camel
Trudging its way by the water mill.
"Let us go and worship the miracle,"
They said, and belted their sheepskin coats.

Their bodies grew warm, walking through snows.
There were footprints that glinted like mica
Across bright fields, on the way to the inn.
But the dogs on seeing the tracks in starshine
Growled loud in anger, as if at a flame.

The frosty night was like a fairy tale.
And phantoms from mountain ridges in snows
Invisibly came to walk in the crowd.
The dogs grew fearful of ghosts around
And huddled beside the shepherd lads.

Across these valleys and mountain roads,
Unbodied, unseen by mortal eyes,

A heavenly host appeared in the throng,
And each footprint gleamed as an angel's foot.

At dawn the cedars lifted their heads.
A multitude clustered around the cave.
"Who are you?" said Mary. They spoke: "We come
As shepherds of flocks, as envoys of heaven:
In praise of the Child and your glory we come."
"There's no room in the cave; you must wait outside."

Before dawnlight, in gloom, in ashen dark,
The drivers and shepherds stamped in the cold.
The footmen quarreled with mounted men;
Near the well and the wooden water trough
The asses brayed and the camels bellowed.

The dawn! It swept the last of the stars
Like flecks of ash from the vaulted sky.
Then Mary allowed the Magi alone
To enter the cleft of the mountainside.

He slept in His manger in radiant light,
As a moonbeam sleeps in a hollow tree.
The breath of the ox and the ass kept warm
His hands and feet in the cold of night.

The Magi remained in the twilight cave;
They whispered softly, groping for words.
Then someone in darkness touched the arm
Of one near the manger, to move him aside:
Behold, like a guest above the threshold,
The Star of the Nativity gazed on the Virgin.

DAYBREAK

You were all my life, my destiny.
Then came the war and ruin, too,
And for a long, long time I had
No sign, no scrap of news from you.

And now I hear your warning voice
Across the years of grief and pain.
At night I read your Testament
And rouse myself to life again.

I long to be with people, crowds,
To share their morning animation,
Prepared to bring them to their knees,
To smash to bits their desolation.

And so each morning I run down
The stairs, at breakneck speed below,
As though this were my first release
To long deserted streets in snow.

The lights come on in cozy rooms.
Men drink their tea, and hurry down
To trolley lines. Within an hour
You'd hardly recognize the town.

The snows are weaving thick and low
Their silver nets above the street.
Men hurry on to get to work
And hardly take their time to eat.

My heart goes out to each and all,
To everyone who feels he's down;
Myself I melt as melts the snow,
And as the morning frowns, I frown.

As women, children, or even as trees,
The nameless are all a part of me.
They've won me over, and by that sign
I know my sole true victory.

THE MIRACLE

He walked to Jerusalem from Bethany
With forebodings and grief in His heart.

The thorny brushwood lay scorched by the sun.
No smoke from a hut or a hostelry near;
No breeze in the reeds. And the air hung hot
And moveless in space by the quiet Dead Sea.

With a few small clouds in fellowship,
He wearily walked in the dust of the day
With bitter sorrow as of the sour sea
To be with His own disciples again.

There deep in loneliness, brooding, He moved.
The desert smelled in sadness of wormwood.
The world lay still. He stood in the midst
Of the desert alone. The land lay prostrate
As though in a swoon. The heat, the desert,
Dry springs, and lizards wearied His mind.

He beheld a fig tree rise in the way,
With branches and leaves, but He found no fruit.
And He said unto it: "Of what profit thou?
What joy can I have in thy fruitless life?

"I hunger and thirst, but thou art barren.
Thy greeting is worse than stumbling on stone.
How empty, how senseless thy life in my sight!
Stay barren forever to the end of time."

A shudder ran down the tree at that curse,
As a spark of lightning runs down a rod.
And the fig tree instantly withered to ash.

But if roots and trunk, if branches and leaves
Had had their freedom and choice at that hour,
Then nature's laws might have come to their aid.

But a miracle is a miracle—the sign of God:
In a world of chaos, we stand, unprepared,
When it suddenly shines in glory and might.

THE EARTH

Spring rushes like a roaring tide
In Moscow streets and rows of homes.
The moths come fluttering from closets
And settle into summer clothes.
The furs are packed away in trunks.

Along the wooden balconies
Bright flowerpots appear in rows
With stock and gillyflowers.
Rooms have the free-and-easy look
And attics smell of pollen dust.

The alleys shout hail-fellow greetings
To every mole-eyed window frame.
White night and sunset by the river
Just cannot keep their love apart.

And one can hear in the corridors
What's going on all day outside,
Or overhear gay April gossip
In secret with the dripping eaves.
She knows a thousand, thousand stories
About plain people and their sorrows.
Sunrise and evening red grow chill
While wasting time beside the fence.

Each living room and free outdoors
Proclaim this daytime fear and glow,
When the very air feels not the same.
All as one the lacy willow twigs;
As one the burgeoning white buds
At crossroads, on the window sills,
In workshops, and in sunny streets.

Then why do the vistas weep in mist?
Why sour the smell of soil and dung?
But that's just what my call is for—
To keep the miles of great outdoors
And the land outside the city bounds
From grieving in their loneliness!

And so for this in the early spring
My friends and I agree to meet,
Why evening parties are farewells,
Why friendly feasts are testaments—
That the secret springs of suffering
May revive the freezing forms of life.

EVIL DAYS

When He came into Jerusalem
In the week before the feast,
He was hailed by crowds with palms
And hosannas to His glory.

But days grew frightful, grim;
Men's eyebrows knit with scorn,
Their hearts unmoved by love.
And soon came the evil end.

The heavens lay heavy as lead,
Crushing the blocks of houses.
The Pharisees came for proof,
And wheedled like sly old foxes.

He was thrown to the city scum
By powers supporting the Temple.
With the selfsame zeal they had praised
His name, they cursed Him at last.

The rabble from every square
Gathered to peer in the gateways;
They jostled forward and backwards
And waited for the end to come.

The alleys whispered their tales
And the squares their secret talk.
He remembered the flight to Egypt
And His childhood as if in a dream.

He remembered the silent desert,
The majestic mountain top
Where Satan had tempted Him
With kingdoms in all the world.

And the marriage feast at Cana,
And the guests who gazed in awe,
And the sea whereon He had walked
To the boat as across dry land.

And the poor who met in a hovel,
His descent to the vault with a light—
How the candle died down in fear
When Lazarus rose from the dead.

MARY MAGDALENE I

Come night, my devil stands for sure
Beside me. That's the price, the score
I pay for all my days of lust.
Dark memories tear me all to pieces
When I, a slave to the whims of men,
Lived like a fiend, a wanton fool,
Whose only hang-out was the street.

I've now a few scant minutes left
Before the silence of the tomb,
Before the end. But while there's time
I'll shatter at Thy feet my life
Like an alabaster vase of doom.

O what could my existence mean
To me, my Master, my Redeemer,
If Eternity was not the life
Waiting each night for me at home,
Like a late new customer lured
Into the meshes of my craft.

But, pray, explain what sin amounts to
And death and hell and brimstone fire
If I, as everyone can tell,
Became through faith a part of Thee,

Like a branch now grafted to a tree
By the boundless sorrows of my life.

When I embrace Thy feet, O Jesus,
And hold them dear upon my knees,
I'm learning to embrace, perhaps,
The wooden beam, Thy Cross in death,
And, fainting, strain Thee to myself,
And prepare Thy body for the tomb.

MARY MAGDALENE II

Come spring, the womenfolk clean house,
Preparing for the holy Feast.
With myrrh, aloof from everyone,
I will anoint Thy most pure feet.

I'm looking everywhere to find
Thy sandals. I'm blinded by my tears.
My hair has fallen like a pall
In loosened coils and blind my eyes.

I have placed Thy feet upon my skirt
And washed them, Jesus, with my tears.
I wound my necklace round Thy feet;
I dried, I hid them with my hair.

I see the future clearly now
As if the world has come to a stop,
And I can prophesy events
Like an ancient sibyl in a trance.

The veil will tremble in the Temple,
While we will huddle, crouch in fear.
The earth will rock beneath our feet
Perhaps from pity just for me.

The watchmen will be changed again,
And horsemen will be riding by.
A whirlwind, springing in a storm,
Thy Cross will strive to reach the sky.

I'll fall before it, faint beside
The Crucifix. I'll gnaw my lips.
Thy arms, O Lord, upon the Cross
Embrace too many in the world.

For whom Thy life, Thy open arms?
For whom such agony, such power?
Are there so many souls to save,
So many hamlets, rivers, woods?

Three days of agony shall pass,
Three days of frightful emptiness,
But with my faith I shall behold
The hour of Resurrection come.

GARDEN OF GETHSEMANE

The turn along the road was shining bright
In the regardless glimmer of distant stars.
The road circled round the Mount of Olives,
And lower, in the valley, the Kedron ran.

A narrow meadow steeply dipped halfway,
And at its end the Milky Way began.
The silvery grey olives, straining forth,
Appeared to stride upon the empty air.

Beyond the field lay someone's garden plot.
He left His disciples by a stone wall, saying:
"My soul is sorrowful, even unto death;
Tarry outside to keep the watch with me."

He had refused, at His free will, the power
Of miracles and of dominion over life,
As though such powers were granted for a time,
And now he was a mortal, even as a man.

The boundless space of night seemed as a span
Of non-existence and annihilation.
The universal sphere was like a soundless waste
And only the garden spot was warm with life.

And, gazing far into the black abyss
All void, without beginning or an end,
He prayed, the while His body sweated blood:
"My Father, let this cup pass from me."

He eased His mortal weariness with prayer.
He left the garden. He came to His disciples.
He found them in the wayside grass, asleep,
Their eyes grown heavy and their bodies weak.

He wakened them: "God granted life to you
While I am in the world, yet you sprawl like dead.
Behold, the hour is at hand, and the Son of Man
Betrays Himself into the hands of sinners."

And while He spoke, there suddenly appeared
A throng of slaves, a mob of vagrant men,
With swords and torches, with Judas at their head
And a traitor's kiss upon his lips.

Then Peter drew his sword and smote the ruffians;
He struck a servant, cutting off his ear.
But Jesus said: "Put up your sword again.
The way of life is not the way of steel.

"Do you think my Father could not send
In my defense His hosts of winged legions?
My enemies would flee before my face
And never harm a hair upon my head.

"Behold, the book of life is open at a page
Of greater price than the holies of the past.
The written words shall be fulfilled at last.
So be it! Let the future come. Amen.

"The course of ages is like a parable,
And in the passing each may burst in flame.
In the name of their awesome majesty I will,
In my voluntary passion, suffer death.

"I will suffer death and on the third day rise,
And, as rafts come floating down a river,
Like a caravan of sails, the centuries
Will come to me for judgement from the dark."

The poems published in this book were taken
from POEMS by Boris Pasternak (Antioch Press),
translated from the Russian by Eugene M. Kayden
and revised by him for this special Crown edition.
The order of the poems is Boris Pasternak's.

Designed by Frances Yamashita
Set in Romanee, a 20th century typeface
designed by Jan van Krimpen of Holland.
Romanee was created to accompany
the only surviving italic of the 17th century
typefounder Christoffel Van Dijck.
Printed on Hallmark Eggshell Book paper.